THE
ULTIMATE
Guide
TO
EXCEEDING
CUSTOMER
EXPECTATIONS

BRAD WORTHLEY

www.BradWorthley.com

ISBN 0-9770668-0-0

The Ultimate Guide to Exceeding Customer Expectations

© 2005 Brad Worthley

To contact the author for interviews, speaking engagements or book, Video, DVD, CD sales:

Brad Worthley International

12819 SE 38th Street #375

Bellevue, Washington 98006

425-957-9696

Please visit our website at www.BradWorthley.com

Book design by Julie Howell of Studiojules.com

Published by Genesis Publishing, Bellevue, Washington

Printed in the United States of America

Contents

BEING OPEN
TO NEW IDEAS
IS A UNIVERSAL
STRENGTH OF
THE TRULY
SUCCESSFUL

Introduction

Y OU CAN NO LONGER SIMPLY MEET CUSTOMERS' EXPECTATIONS; you must exceed them. This book will help separate you from your competition by allowing you to reap the benefits from your commitment to service excellence. The fact that you purchased this book, already tells me something about you; you're willing to learn new things.

The hardest thing about creating new habits is we have to unlearn old habits and that can be challenging. No matter how much you would like to change, your brain is going to fight you and try to convince you to revert back to your old ways.

In order to help you create positive new habits, I would suggest highlighting portions of this book that are important to you, and then re-reading those sections every two weeks for the next two months. Stay strong, and remember that being open to new ideas is a universal strength of the truly successful.

IN ORDER TO
ACHIEVE GREATNESS
IN THIS WORLD,
YOU MUST HAVE
AN EMPOWERING
SET OF BELIEFS

1
There is Nothing You Have to Do But Die

IBELIEVE IN ORDER TO ACHIEVE GREATNESS IN THIS WORLD, you must have an empowering set of beliefs. Greatness can take many forms, and for everyone, it can look different. If you look at truly successful people, they empowered themselves with some form of belief that motivated them to achieve success and greatness.

The first time I was exposed to an empowering set of beliefs was in 1983, when I was in retail management. I was an operations manager for a small clothing chain with seven stores. We were having a problem with the employees at one store, so our company president and I went to the store to have a meeting with all of the employees. The president had all the employees sit on the floor in a semi-circle, and then he comfortably seated himself in a chair in front of the employees and spoke in a calm and eloquent manner.

He said, "Do you realize that there is nothing you have to do but die?" He challenged the employees to come up with anything they felt they "had to do," and they responded with a list of things such as:

- You have to pay your taxes
- You have to eat
- You have to breathe
- You have to go to school

And one of the employees said,"We had to come to this meeting."

He responded, "You didn't have to come to this meeting; that was a choice that you made freely."

Of course the employee responded back with, "I had to come, because the manager said it was mandatory and I had to be here."

The president calmly told the employee that he certainly had a choice to either come to the meeting and participate with the other employees, or not come to the meeting and risk possible disciplinary action. He told the employee, "Either way, it was a choice that was available to you and congratulations, you made a great choice to show up."

He went through their list one at a time and had them respond as to whether they had the freedom of choice in each circumstance. They did not have to pay their taxes, but if they "chose" not to, they may end up going to jail. They did not have to eat, but if they "chose" not to, they might die from starvation. They did not have to breathe, but if they "chose" not to, then they would certainly die. They never had to go to school, but if they "chose" not to, they would not get an education, and more than likely find it hard to find a job; they may end up broke and with no way to feed themselves it could eventually lead to death.

AWARENESS WILL CREATE CHANGE

They acknowledged that even though there were potential consequences for making a bad choice, they truly did have choices in every circumstance. It made me and all of the other employees in that room, realize that we had always been totally empowered to make choices freely. We were certainly aware that there could be consequences for our choices, but the fact that no one could "make us" come to work, serve customers, and do as we are told, was powerful and freeing. When we came to work the next day, it was because we "chose" to do it. When we worked hard, it was because we "chose" to do so. When we happily served our customers, it was because we "chose" to do so.

I have never forgotten the lesson or the message, and it has guided me through many emotionally challenging times. Reflecting back, it removed the victim mentality that so many of the employees possessed. Before the talk, they were caught up in the "I have to" mode of their job responsibilities, which was emotionally debilitating and kept them from greatness. That mode rendered them emotional victims and kept them small in this large world of opportunity. If you hear an employee, co-worker, friend or family member use those words, tell them the story above and challenge them to think of things they "have to do." If you hear yourself think or say those words, then slap yourself silly, because now you know better: Awareness will create change!

2
No One Can *Make You*
Do Anything

BEING GREAT AT CUSTOMER SERVICE AND LEARNING TO EXCEED
the customers' expectations is something that so many
employees are told to do, but very few ever achieve it. First,
you have to want that as your chosen goal and not have it
thrust upon you by someone else. One of your empowering
set of beliefs could be that no one can "make you" do anything. If you truly believe that outside forces control your
life, then you are a victim and this book will never help you.
Matter of fact, I will venture to say that there isn't any book
that can help you, so save yourself the reading time.

I drive myself nuts when I hear anyone use words like:
- They make me angry
- They make me sad
- They make me jealous
- They make me crazy
- They make me happy
- They made me do it
- They confused me
- They drive me nuts

Now, if you look at the way I started the last paragraph, you can see that I said: "I drive myself nuts..." (Instead of saying "they drive me nuts" or "it drives me nuts"). Do you see how I took full responsibility for my feelings? I accepted the fact that the emotion and action is generated by me and no one else.

Nobody can "make you" anything, because no one should be given that much power. If somebody "makes you angry," it is because you allowed them to take over your emotions (actually, you voluntarily gave it up). They cannot control your emotions unless you grant them that power, and I highly recommend that you never grant anyone that much power.

Whether it is personal relationships or in the business world, I want you to always be aware that you are the only one in control of your emotions. If you get angry, sad, jealous, crazy, happy, or nuts, it is because you make the conscious decision to choose that emotion. If you did choose that emotion, was it a good choice for you and did it serve you well? If not, then I challenge you to review your choice and make another choice that empowers you and keeps you in control.

In the world of customer service, you will encounter those who will try to take away your power. They will do so by trying to challenge, intimidate, or antagonize you, which if successful can feed their power even more. If you let these people impact your life, then everyone comes out a loser (you, them, co-workers, and other customers). However, if you can impact their lives, keep yourself and them calm, and handle the situation in a professional manner, everyone wins.

3
Creatures of Habit

REMEMBER, THE WHOLE IDEA BEHIND AN EMPOWERING set of beliefs is to empower you and give you choices in your life. It is about the conscious decision to not let anyone else gain control over you, no matter how hard they may try. Is this easy? Of course not! Look how long some of you have allowed yourselves to be emotional hostages. You may have developed a negative habit, and habits are not easy to rid yourself of, so it may take time. As you go through each day, old habits will be challenging you and trying to get you to revert back to your old ways. When this happens, you will have to recognize and learn to manage them. Habits can come in the form of behavior, thinking, feelings, or perceptions. They lie below the surface; under our level of awareness, and they certainly impact our daily lives.

A Tibetan Buddhist Rinpoche named Chogyam Trungpa once wrote: "No one is more arrogant than someone who is caught up in habits, that they cannot understand how another person can interpret things in a different way, or can desire to do something different." Successful people sometimes get caught up in the arrogance of habits, which can work against them in the long run. If your habits have created success for you in the past, then your brain tries to keep you using those same habits. However, times change, and people need to change with those times. Relying on past habits for future success can lead to habits that make you lethargic or complacent. Being open to new ideas and new ways of doing things is a universal strength of the truly successful.

Changing habits is difficult because our brain is constantly monitoring inbound information, and trying to protect us from pain. Our brain is our friend, and it is trying to work in our best interest. But when it comes to breaking habits, it is our worst enemy. As our brain monitors our thoughts and other inbound information, it is seeking to protect us from either physical or emotional pain. It is certainly our friend when it is trying to protect us from physical pain, so it throws up flags of caution from time to time to keep us safe. But in its effort to protect us from emotional pain, it becomes overzealous and keeps us from sometimes making positive changes.

Emotional pain can be:
- Embarrassment
- Sadness
- Guilt
- Rejection
- Fear
- Failure

To keep us safe from these pains, our brain will send us messages that try to drive us back into our comfort zone. When we are taught how to do something new, our brain will react and say; "This isn't the way we normally do this – let's do it our way because it is safe." Most of our brains are not risk takers, and work very hard to keep us doing things the same way, even if they are wrong. Even if our current way is painful, our brain is tolerant of the pain because there are no surprises (it knows what to expect). It is the fear of the unknown and the unexpected that encourages our brain to send warning signals and drive us back to the safety of our old habits.

When you try some of the suggestions in this book, listen very carefully to your "self-talk" because it will probably be trying to drive you back to your old behaviors. In order to experience how challenging change is, try this exercise: Hold both hands straight out in front of your body and spread your fingers apart. Now press the palms of your hands together, and weave your fingers in the process (hands should be clasped), like you are going to do the old "church and steeple" game that you may have done as a child.

Notice which fingers are on top of each other: If you are right handed, you would normally have your left thumb laying over your right thumb, and the same with your index finger and the rest of your fingers (left handed people will more than likely have their right fingers on top). Now unclasp your hands and pull them apart about two feet, then quickly put them back to together again, BUT THIS TIME, do it so the opposite fingers are on top as you weave them together.

Did you have to think about it real hard? Did your brain try to stop you from doing it the new way, and drive you back to the old way? If your brain works so hard to keep you from making simple changes in your life like this, think how hard it will work to keep you from making big and important changes.

Your self-talk can take a long time to go away, and sometimes it never goes away. In order to be successful in change, you need to manage your self-talk and be aware it is speaking to you. I believe that awareness creates change, and if you are aware of your self-talk, then you can manage your change much more successfully.

I also relate habits to other addictions in our lives, like alcohol, drugs, coffee, chocolate, foods, and other things that our bodies crave. In many cases, even with awareness, the cravings don't simply go away. We will have to find a way to manage these habits or addictions. I believe that many people are also addicted to giving up their power, and find comfort in doing so. As long as these people believe that other people control their lives, then they can continue to play the victim role that suits them so well. Life can actually be simpler for victims because there aren't many decisions they have to make. And if others are making the decisions in their life, then it reduces the chance of them ever having to be wrong. Life is sweet, because anything that goes wrong in their life was certainly someone else's fault.

4
This Job Isn't For Everyone

IF YOU WANT TO BE GREAT AT CUSTOMER SERVICE and learn to exceed customer expectations, you are going to want to choose to serve all customers. You cannot pick and choose who you want to serve. Will this be easy every day? Of course not, because life is not that simple. So graciously embrace the great days and be thankful the bad days are few and far between.

When I speak of "customers," I want you to understand who these customers are. They are the external-customer that walks through the door, or calls you on the telephone and asks you to assist them with their needs. They are also the internal-customer, which are our co-workers, supervisors, and people within our organization that we might serve. They can be the accounting department, which handles the paperwork for the sales department. It can be the print shop that serves the marketing department. It can be the mailroom that serves every employee and department within the company, or it can be the person that works right next to you on the sales floor who helps locate merchandise, answers difficult questions, handles irate customers or helps you close the sale in a team effort.

Customers come in all shapes and sizes, and can also come in many different emotional packages. They will be sweet, and make your day a complete joy. Or they will drop you to your knees crying with their abusive attitudes. It is Russian roulette out there, and in most cases, you cannot pick your customers, you simply get what you get. Understanding this and accepting this as reality, is your first step to success. I did not say you had to like it, I simply said you have to accept this as reality and the truth.

If this is not acceptable to you, then I would highly recommend that you find a profession where you do not work with humans. This does not mean you are not a nice person, or that there is anything wrong with you, it simply means you are not cut out for the world of customer service. So be authentic with yourself and make sure that you have chosen the right job for you. Part of empowerment is the ability to accept who and what you are, and embrace it. Celebrate who you are, and don't put yourself into jobs where you are setting yourself up for failure. Understanding that you do not enjoy serving people is a huge disclosure and you should congratulate yourself for your authenticity.

5
Happiness – Grab All You Can

N OW THAT WE HAVE BEEN AUTHENTIC WITH OURSELVES and have "chosen" to work with customers, we need to go back to the discussion about not allowing anyone to control our emotions. With that said, since you have been so good about your choice to read this book so far, I will grant you one emotional freedom; happiness. If a customer wants to spread happiness to you, then reach out and grab as much as you can. Matter of fact, be unreasonable, and ask for more! These customers are sometimes few and far between. So let their happiness infect you and thank them for sharing. It is also the time to reciprocate, because they have brought you the fabulous gift to share, and the least we can do is offer them a big slice in return.

The number one motivator for people is recognition or praise. Do not let this customer leave your world without letting them know how their happiness has made your day. This is not the time to be shy; it is the time to let loose and be verbal! Let them know how their smile and attitude has made your day better and how much you appreciate their unconditional gift. If you don't know this already, then you should know it now: "Praise breeds change." If you praise people for their positive behavior it will, in most cases, breed more positive change. Hand it out in buckets and watch what you get back in return. Praise is a huge annuity, with a large return on your investment.

Every company that I am aware of that has a great service-culture, has found one thing to be very true; the better you treat the customer, the better they will treat you in return. The annuity in exceeding the customer's expectations is massive, and is a proactive approach to enjoying your work. If you consistently treat the customer well, then if they ever have a problem or an issue, they will more than likely approach you with respect and courtesy. Why would the customer want to show their fangs to someone who has treated them so well in the past? The energy you put out today in exceeding the customer's expectations will pay you back handsomely in the future.

6
Bad Hair Days

NOW, FOR THE OTHER SIDE OF THE FENCE: We will encounter customers who can quicken our pulse, make us go pale, send shivers down our spine, go weak in the knees, make our blood boil, and cause many other physical transformations. This, by the way, is not a matter of "if," it is a matter of "when." Some of these customers do not intentionally mean to do this to us, but there are others who come to the party with the intention to do us harm.

I truly believe that most customers who allow us to create high anxiety in ourselves (remember, no one can give us anxiety, we give it to ourselves), simply want empathy, to be heard, and want solutions to their problems. They don't want to fight with you and they don't want you mad at them. But in many cases our past dictates our future, so some customers, remembering a past experience in dealing with a similar situation, get hostile in preparation for the perceived battle they think they are in for. These people will come at you with their fangs out because they want to show you who the big dog on the block is, and how they are not going to be kicked all the way back to the porch.

Then, there are the "controllers," who will come at you with all guns blazing, even with the smallest of problems, because they want to show you who is in control. By the way, this is not about you - it is all about them. Do not take their aggressive interaction or attacks personally, because in most cases, they were not seeking you out specifically, you just happen to be the first one to the scene of the accident. This is their life and this is the way they are with everyone, including family and friends. When I have encountered these people in my life, my first thought is: "Boy, I am glad I am not married to you."

It does not make any difference whether it is the customer who wants solutions or the controller who loves to see you sweat; you need to always remain in control of your own emotions. They will try to intrude on your emotional space, and the controller will thrive on taking over your emotions. Do not let that happen under any circumstance. Take a deep breath; remind yourself that you are in charge and in control of your emotions, not them. Focus on the goal of solving their perceived problem, find the shortest path to that goal and do not get caught up in the emotional moment.

Once again, this will not be easy, because as humans, when we are pushed, we want to push back. Your mind is going to be screaming: "I would like to kick their butt all the way to the door!" But do not let yourself get pulled over to the dark side. Yes, think of Star Wars and remember that if you let the customer take control of your emotions, everyone loses. If you let them pull you over to the dark side, then you have given up your freedom, and surrendered to their power. Stand your emotional ground and keep calm no matter how painful it is feeling. You might feel like you need to get angry back in order to show them how powerful you are. WRONG! This only shows them how weak you are. The true power is in your control and in your ability to not let your decision making skills get washed away with your emotions.

7
Giving Lip Service to Customer Service

ONE OF MY PEEVES IS WHEN I HEAR A BUSINESS on the radio touting, "We've got great customer service, come on down and visit us today!" You know what; chances are they are paying that statement lip service. The worst thing you can do to your business is to tell people how great you are, and then not deliver as promised. Customers won't be very forgiving because they will feel like you lied to them, or tried to manipulate them. Even if you didn't do it on purpose, you will still leave that perception.

If you are going to promise great service, the consistency at which you offer that service must be impeccable. You have no room for "bad hair days" and moments of less than glory. Each day and each customer must get 100% of your best, or you will under-whelm your customers. In fact, you should probably do the opposite: You should under-promise, and then over-deliver in order to exceed the customer's expectations. Tell your customers; "We have the worst service in town, come on down and see!" Obviously, I am kidding, but my point is about not promising great service unless you are truly ready to deliver it to each and every customer.

What questions do customers ask themselves when they're deciding where to spend their hard earned money? Here is the process that most people go through: Let's just say you wanted to buy a big screen television. The first thing you're going to ask yourself is: "Who has big screen TVs?" This will help you narrow your choices down to maybe 5 businesses that are in your area. The second thing you're going to ask yourself is "Who has the best price or the best value for my money?" And, the third thing is: "Where am I going to get the best service?" And that's where your decision making power presents itself.

This is especially true in commoditized industries like retail, restaurants and banking. Service can dictate where we're going to spend our money. A lot of businesses have the same "stuff," and a lot of businesses have about the same prices, so it is hard to separate yourself from the competition. The only way you can differentiate yourself today, in most cases, is with the level of service that you offer. That is one of the big determining factors on where we consumers are going to spend our money.

8

Exceeding Customer Expectations

IN ORDER TO EXCEED CUSTOMER EXPECTATIONS, and not just meet them, you really need to think outside of the box. You may be sick of hearing about "thinking outside the box," but that box I'm talking about is an emotional box. Most of us who have been doing our job for any length of time have developed a routine of doing it the same way. We just stay inside of that comfortable box and do our job over and over and over again the same way each day because it is safe. If you're going to exceed people's expectations, you've got to step out of that box. You've got to do some things that you have never done before. I truly believe that with the biggest risks come the biggest rewards. So even though there is emotional risk to stepping out and doing new things, I think you're going to find that the rewards outweigh the risks many times over.

I want to give you some examples of retail businesses that have stepped out of that box and done some things that most other businesses are not willing to do, and some of the paybacks they have gotten for doing so. And also, what the rewards were for the employees who worked for those companies.

One of the first businesses I would like to talk about is an organization called Les Schwab Tire Centers. As of the writing of this book, Les Schwab has about 400 locations in the far Western States. Many years ago, Les Schwab himself decided to get on TV and do something that nobody else was going to do. He decided to give away "free beef" for buying tires from him. Yes, you heard me, "free beef." Now, I've got to admit I had never been to a Les Schwab Tire Center until about 10 years ago. I was driving down the street and had a flat tire. I looked across the street and there was a Les Schwab Tire Center. I had seen Les on TV for probably 35 years with his white cowboy hat and his rancher outfit on, telling the world; "You buy tires from me, I'll give you beef right out of my freezer!" And they do! So, I decided I would have the beef guy fix my tire for me. I pulled in, and they fixed my tire for me. I went up to the counter to pay, pulled out my wallet, and I said, "How much do I owe you?"

They said, "Mr. Worthley, we don't want your money today, all we want you to do is consider us for your future tire purchases."

I felt guilty and said, "No, really, how much do I owe you?"

And, they said, "No, really, Mr. Worthley, all we want you to do, is think about us the next time you're looking for tires."

I was shocked! Whoever gave you anything for free, especially in the automotive industry? It was nuts! And, you know what, they didn't get their $9 or $10 that day, but over the last 10 years, they've got eight or nine thousand of my dollars. Anything that goes wrong with my car or my life, I call Les. They are a great organization.

There are other things that they do to exceed their customer's expectations. Yes, they do give away free beef if you buy tires during certain promotions. They will also change anybody's flat tire for free, and you don't have to be a customer of the Les Schwab Tire Centers (however, you will be a customer once you deal with them). If you want the air pressure in your tires checked, they'll do that for you and normally won't charge you a dime. If you want your tires rotated, chances are they'll do that for free as well whether you are a customer or not (it is part of their guaranteed service if you are a customer). All of the Les Schwab Tire Centers have fresh popcorn being cooked all day long, and yes, it is free! They also have fresh coffee available in all of their locations, and yes, it is also free!

Every time I do a seminar in a town where there is a Les Schwab Tire center, someone has a great story about something outrageous that they did. One woman told me how she had a flat tire and went in to have it repaired. They told her the tire was ruined and it could not be fixed. She told them she did not have enough money for new tires right now and asked if they could put a used tire on her car until she gets paid. The gentleman waiting on her asked her to wait a minute and then he disappeared into the work area. He came back about 10 minutes later, handed her the keys to her car and said it was ready. She walked to her car with the young man and found a brand new tire on her car where she had previously had the flat. In shock, she told the gentleman that she could not afford a new tire, and he told her there would be no charge. He simply invited her to come back when she was ready to replace the three other worn tires, which she did.

A young college student who attended one of my seminars said that there was a Les Schwab Tire center in her small farming town in Oregon. Her family had been loyal Les Schwab customers for over twenty five years, but times had been tough due to a couple of bad farming seasons. It was a snowy winter, and she was leaving for college, and had a long drive ahead. She stopped by Les Schwab to buy tire chains for her trip, but they noticed that her tires were worn so badly, that they had very little tread. They told her of the problem, but she told them that the family could barely afford to send her to college and they did not have enough money for new tires. They asked her to have a seat and cup of coffee. Thirty minutes later, they presented her with her tire chains and four brand new tires for free. She thanked them profusely for their incredible gift, and in return, they thanked her and her family for their years of loyal business.

These are the kinds of things that are not covered in policy manuals. Even though employees need guidelines, the main policy should also be: "Do everything you can to exceed the customer's expectations." So, did all of these incredible services and great ideas happen overnight? Of course not, these are things that happened over time. Les Schwab owns the business in every town they're in; they dominate the industry wherever they are. So what inspires a company like this to keep raising the service bar? This is the big message I want you to get. No matter how good you are today, you can never stop trying to wow the customer and exceed their expectations. You should always have a plan in place each year to continue to raise that service bar and find ways to make the customer go "Wow! That's incredible!" And, that is something that Les Schwab does better than anybody, in any industry.

Les Schwab took their service to an even higher level a few years ago, which really blew me away even more than I already was. I had an appointment to have some brake work done. I turned in to the parking lot one morning, and pulled up to the curb to park. Just so you can get a visual on this, I pulled up to the curb that was facing the street, so the building was behind me. When I pulled up to the curb, I put my car into park. As I did so, I just happened to glance up in my rear view mirror, and noticed a young man who was working on a car outside. He looked up, saw me, dropped his tools, and came running full speed for my car. I have to admit that I thought my car must have been on fire by his urgency. He got to my car, opened up my door, and greeted me warmly. I looked up at him and was thinking to myself;

"This kid has got to be new, or it was his review day or something." I didn't know for sure, but that's not normal behavior. He walked me all the way inside, sat me down and filled out my paperwork. He even brought me a cup of water because I was talking about how warm it was.

Every car that pulled into the parking lot, somebody dropped their tools, and raced for the car. Now, I am trying to

DO WHAT OTHERS AREN'T WILLING TO DO, SO THAT WHEN SOMEONE ASKS WHO YOUR COMPETITION IS, YOU CAN HONESTLY SAY: "WE DON'T HAVE ANY!"

think about who in this organization is sitting around one day saying to themselves; "Let's see, we give away free beef, we offer free tire repair, tire rotation, popcorn, coffee, and we pretty much dominate the business in every town we're in...," what inspired somebody in that organization to say to themselves; "I know, we should start running for that darn car."

That's not normal thinking. That is so far out of the box, that it seems nuts! They also know that none of their competition would be willing to do the same thing, so how smart is that? This is a great lesson: If you want to separate yourself from your competition, you better be willing to do things that they are not willing to do. One of the greatest marketing lessons I ever learned was to make sure you don't have any competition. Do what others aren't willing to do, so when someone asks who your competition is, you can honestly say; "We don't have any!"

Imagine what that must have been like when someone from upper management got up in front of all the managers and said, "Hey everybody, I've got a great idea, let's start running for that darn car." You've got to figure that it didn't go over real big! I actually asked the young man who was waiting on me what that was like when he found out he was going to be running for a car.

He said, "You have got to be kidding. Here I am, trying to get work done; a customer pulls in, what a huge inconvenience this is going to be. I have to drop my tools and run for a car." He said, "That just wasn't good news!" But he also said that after a few days, he found out what was in it for himself, and then it was okay.

I asked, "What was it that you found out?"

"I will tell you that it got to be so darned much fun to run to that car, open the door, and see those customers looking at you with that shocked look on their face - that was a good time! I found that the better I treated the customer, the better they treated me. What a huge payoff," he said, "it was fabulous!"

This is a huge lesson every company and employee needs to learn: The better you treat customers, the better they treat you. If you learn nothing else from this book, that is the one thing you need to get. Exceeding customer's expectations provides a huge annuity; a huge payback over time which allows you to enjoy your job more.

Another organization, Safeway Grocery & Drug, stepped outside the box by creating a simple customer service mission: "Let's start treating customers the way we personally would like to be treated." They decided to do a few new things that no other large grocery store chain was doing consistently. It set them apart from everyone else in the industry and changed the industry because everyone has been trying to duplicate their success ever since.

Prior to the launch of Safeway's new mission, I had been talking to them about hiring my consulting firm to provide mystery shopping services to their organization. For those who are unfamiliar with mystery shopping, I shall explain: We send people into our clients' locations to act like regular customers and have a normal experience. The difference is; the shoppers we send in will report back about their experience. They would complete a questionnaire on the Internet that helps us measure the level of service for our clients. This would occur in every location, every month, and helps us to gauge the effectiveness of hiring, training, systems and procedures. This is still done today by most banks, chain restaurants, hotels, rental car companies, apartment complexes, and many other businesses.

I was trying to convince Safeway to do mystery shopping in their stores, so I had been communicating with them for a few months. I came home one night and my wife, at the time, said "Brad, did you get the Safeway account?"

I said, "No, why?"

"Well," she replied, "Something's going on down at Safeway; I just came from there and something's different."

"What?"

"They were nice."

I laughed, and said, "Okay, let me go down and find out why."

I went down to the Safeway store in my neighborhood, because I had to get some bananas anyhow. I entered the store and I walked over to the produce section. I was reaching for the bananas, and a gentleman walks over to me (for the very first time ever in a grocery store,) and says, "Are you finding everything you're looking for?"

I said, "Yes, I'm just getting some bananas."

"Well, if you don't find exactly what you're looking for, let me know, because I'll go in the back room, and I'll locate it for you."

I told him that I was a customer service consultant, and I asked if there was something new happening at Safeway.

He said, "Well, I'll be honest with you, I've been working at Safeway for 20 years and I'm the Produce Manager. I've seen programs come and programs go, and most of them go away. So, when they introduced a new customer service program, I thought I'm going to let this program go away too, just like the rest. So, initially, I didn't jump on the bandwagon, I just sat back and watched. But all of the other employees did jump in, and I will bet it didn't take 3 weeks, and all of a sudden I saw our customers changing. The customers were walking over to me and saying 'hi.' They were treating me better. That's when I saw the payoff." He added, "I was enjoying my job more, and that is when I decided I would do something new and become part of this new culture."

I said, "What did you start doing?"

"Well, did you hear a second ago, how I asked 'Are you finding everything you're looking for?'"

I said, "Yes, you said that."

"Did you also hear that I said, 'If you could not find exactly what you're looking for, you let me know, because I'll go in the back room and I'll locate it for you.'"

"Yes, you did say that."

"Well, there's nothing in the back room. I brought it all out this morning," he said, "but I want my customers to hear a very important message, which is `If you can't find what you're looking for, I'm willing to go out of my way for you, and locate it,' that's my contribution to this new culture."

If you are walking through a Safeway Store, you can walk through five different departments and you could have five different employees acknowledge you. You can be in produce and they'll say "Good morning." You can walk over to the meat department, and they'll say, "Are you finding everything you're looking for?" You can be acknowledged multiple times in one of these stores. Let's say you do need something, like a can of garbanzo beans. Well, in most grocery stores, they'll point and say, "Oh, that's on Aisle 21." Not in a Safeway Store, because they have a no pointing rule. They'll walk you all the way to that product. And I have actually had them pick up the requested product from the bottom shelf, and hand it to me.

When you get to the cashier, they are supposed to use your name. They will read your name off of your credit card, debit card, check, or your Safeway Card, and they'll use your name most of the time. But, what you may not realize, is the person boxing the groceries is supposed to listen to the cashier use your name, and they're supposed to use it as well. They are not quite as good at that, but you can't get that treatment in most other grocery stores.

Like the day I bought those bananas. The cashier rung them up and I used my Safeway Card to get the discount. She said, "Mr. Worthley, thank you, and have a great day." I turned around and there was a 14-year-old boy standing there, holding a bag with my bananas in it. He said, "Mr. Worthley, may I carry this out for you?" Whether it's a bag or a cart, it doesn't make any difference; they're always going to offer to carry that out for you in order to exceed your expectations.

Most grocery stores look and act alike, and have become a commodity. Safeway stepped out and started doing a few new things that nobody else was doing, and they immediately began to beat their competition. Even the small mom and pop grocery stores were getting killed, because Safeway was doing things that even the mom and pop stores had not been willing to do. Which was offer individualized personalized service and treat the customer the way we all would like to personally be treated. Now, most grocery stores are mystery shopping, and everybody is trying to chase Safeway's success. What a great place to be – where everybody is chasing you. Safeway was successful because they changed their culture and not just their people.

The next company I will talk about is the DoubleTree Inns. I had never stayed in a DoubleTree until about seven years ago. I was in San Diego where one of my large clients hired me to perform seminars at a DoubleTree Inn, and made reservations for me to stay there as well. I had performed more seminars than usual that day, my throat was swollen, plus I was tired and exhausted. I arrived at the check-in desk about 11:30 p.m. that night, with my head almost lying on the counter from exhaustion.

The gentleman behind the desk greets me, checks me in, and hands me my room key. Then he turns around and reaches over to a warming oven. Now, I've seen warming ovens in Mexican restaurants, where they keep the chips warm, but I had never seen one in a hotel lobby before. He reached over, opened up the drawer, and pulled out a bag with two warm chocolate chip cookies inside! (I understand they have now cut back to giving only one cookie as of the publishing of this book.) Now, I don't know about you, but getting two warm chocolate chip cookies at 11:30 at night was a great idea. I didn't even know they were free, but I knew he wasn't getting them back. I got to the elevator, the door opened up, and six people walked out with chocolate all over their faces. I wasn't the only one that thought the cookies were a great idea! Also, at the time of my visit, if there was anything wrong with your room, they would send up 6 warm chocolate chip cookies as compensation – that is also a great unexpected surprise that would exceed most people's expectations.

I want you to think about this - who in that organization came up with that idea? Who was sitting around the office one day saying, "Let's see, we have the Hyatt, Marriott, Hilton, Westin, Sheraton, Radisson and tons of other hotel competition, so what can we do to separate ourselves from the others?" What on earth made that person think to themselves, "I know, cookies! I'll bet cookies would be good, and warm cookies would even be better." This is an organization that is willing to think outside the box.

The day after I came back from my trip to San Diego, I was giving a speech on customer service at the University of Washington. It was to a group of executives from large businesses located all over the United States. I mentioned my experience with the DoubleTree Inns and the free cookies. As I was telling my story, I noticed a table of four executives to the right of me raising their hands and wanting to talk. I stopped my story and asked if they had a question. They said they had also never stayed in a DoubleTree until recently, and that those weren't just cookies, they were good cookies.

They told me they contacted their corporate travel planner, and notified the planner that when they travel, they always want to stay in a DoubleTree Inn so they can get their cookies. Forty cents worth of cookies and you get a $140 a night room – that is a pretty good return on your investment.

The one thing I want you to understand is that outstanding customer service, which exceeds people's expectations, helps create an emotional attachment. I don't care if you ever use the words "customer service" again, because those words have been overused. What I do want you to think about with every single customer is, what are you going to do when a customer walks through the door or in to your department, to create an emotional attachment with them? They should walk out believing that there's no place else they can go, to get that kind of service.

Using the customers' name at Safeway is very powerful for creating an emotional attachment with the customer. Where else are you going to go, besides Les Schwab Tire

Centers, where they are actually going to run to your car to show you how important you are? In order to make your customer go "WOW," are you willing to put warming ovens and chocolate chip cookies into the most unlikely place?

So what are you going to do to step outside of the box? How will your customer have an exceptional experience that exceeds their expectations?

9

Perception is the Customer's Reality

PERCEPTION IS TRULY THE CUSTOMER'S REALITY. Say you're driving down the street trying to find someplace to take your significant-other out to lunch. You pull up in front of a restaurant that you happen to see and take in the view. You can see that the paint is chipped and cracked, and probably hasn't been painted for about 20 years. You look at the windows and see a layer of grease on the inside, where it hasn't been cleaned for a few months. The "OPEN" sign is hanging crooked in the window with old scotch tape all over it. The front door has finger prints all over it, so you know it has not been cleaned for a while either.

Now, are you going to go in there and eat? I don't know about you, but my perception is; if you can't take care of the stuff that I can see, what are you doing to the stuff that I can't see? And that would worry me. My perception is that the place is a dump. I'm not eating there and I'll drive on. Now, the reality might be that the food is fabulous. Maybe they spent all of their money on the inside, on the kitchen or the interior décor. It may be fabulous on the inside, but my perception became my reality, and I moved on.

Say you are nearing retirement and want to find a financial advisor to assist you in investing your life savings in order to provide you with a comfortable retirement. You looked in the yellow pages under financial advisors and found a colorful, professional ad that promised great results. You call and make an appointment, drive 20 minutes to the office, and walk in the door. Once inside, you notice that the reception desk has papers stacked about a foot tall all over it, and there are boxes spread out against the wall

BE AWARE OF WHAT CUSTOMERS COULD MISPERCEIVE

as storage. The filing cabinets are so full, that most of the drawers don't close. The financial advisor comes out to meet you and his hair has not been combed for a few days, and his clothes are wrinkled and not clean. He offers you a seat, but has to move the file folders from the only chair in the office and you can hardly see his face through the pile of paper on his desk as well. As you look around the office, all you see is disorganization.

What is your perception? Do you really want to turn your life savings over to this person? The question I would ask myself is: "If they can't take care of themselves, and organize their own offices, are they going to be able to organize my finances and take care of me?" There is no way I would hand someone my life savings so they can disorganize it too. Is it fair of me to judge this person that way? Is my perception wrong? Of course my perception is not wrong, because it is my perception: Yours might be different, but that is the good news and bad news about perception; it is each person's reality.

Let's look at another example. You walk into a bank branch which is very busy and there are 20 customers lined up waiting for a teller. You notice that there are 3 teller windows in this branch, but there are only 2 tellers who are actually working in the windows. However, there is a third person that is working behind the tellers doing some other miscellaneous work. Guess who all 20 people in line are all staring at? Do you think they're staring at the two tellers who are working and bringing the line down? Of course not; they're looking at the third person behind the tellers, wondering, "What is that other person doing ignoring us? Since there is a window available, how come that person can't come over and help bring the line down? If that person is qualified to be behind the tellers, they must be qualified to be one of them." The customer will punish you emotionally for that internal conversation they are having with themselves about their perceptions.

And, guess what else is happening? The two tellers who are working diligently to help bring that line down are wondering to themselves why all the customers are in such bad moods. They can't figure it out, and maybe they even treat the customers poorly in return. Well, the reason the customers are in a bad mood, is because they've had about 15 minutes to stand in line and look at that one person who they perceived as indifferent towards helping bring the line down. This generated all sorts of anxiety, and the two tellers that get punished by the waiting customers are the ones that are working as hard as they can. Perception is not always fair.

I have a story for you from a great book called Sandbox Wisdom by Tom Asacker. There's a cute story in there that I shall just paraphrase. It's about a grandfather driving around a small town with his granddaughter one day. She asks her grandfather if they can stop and buy some candy. The grandfather agreed, so they drive downtown to find the candy store. The grandfather pulls up downtown, and to his surprise, there's a candy store on the right side and a candy store on the left side of the street.

So the grandfather asks his granddaughter, "Which store do you kids go to get your candy?"

And, she says, "We always go to the one on the right side of the street, because she gives us extra candy."

"What about the one on the left side of the street?"

"Oh, we don't go in there, she takes candy away from us."

The grandfather thought that was kind of odd, but proceeded to pull over in front of the store of his granddaughter's choosing.

He orders a half-pound of hard candy, and the nice lady takes a small scoop of the candy and puts it up on the scale. She then reaches in to the bin and she grabs small handfuls of candy, and puts them up on the scale to bring it up to a half pound. She takes that candy, dumps it into a bag, and hands it to the young girl with a smile, and they left the store. The grandfather, out of curiosity, decides to go across the street and go to the other candy store to see what that place was like. He walks in, orders half pound of the exact same hard candy. The lady seemed very nice too as she took a big scoop of the hard candy and put it up on the scale. She then reached up onto the scale and grabbed small handfuls of the candy to remove them from the scale in order to bring it down to half a pound. Now, did anybody do anything wrong? Of course not, but look at the different perceptions that were created by their actions.

What is it that you do every day in your job or your task that creates misperceptions about some of the things that you're doing. Stand back and take a look at your place of business, and look at the exterior and surrounding area. Are there cigarette butts, pop cans, paper and other debris in the parking lot that have gone unnoticed? Does the outside of the building look tired, run down and un-maintained? Did a tree that you planted 10 years ago grow up and cover the sign to your business? Is your work station or desk meticulous and clean? What do all of these things mean to your customers? Could they perceive that your lack of attention to detail could be reflective in your business performance as well?

Take a look at your work area, look at yourself, and look at all of that from the customer's perspective. That's what I call, T. L. C. "Think Like a Customer." Be aware of what customers could misperceive. For those who find it challenging to remove yourself from your business and look at it objectively; ask family, friends, or other people who will be honest with you. Ask if you can borrow their eyes, so that you can see yourself and your business from the customer's perspective. There also may be things that are not as obvious to you or your friends, because they are behaviors that have become unwilling habits. These behaviors may be under your radar screen, but not the customers'.

As an example, if you are at a used car dealership looking to buy a car and the salesperson is not looking at you in the eyes as he is talking; what perception might you be left with? Are you questioning their integrity? Are you wondering whether the salesperson is lacking confidence in himself or his products? Both of these perceptions may or may not be true, but they become our reality, and can impact our decision to purchase.

Let's say you are trying to locate a commercial banker to handle your business account. You have narrowed it down to two different companies based on recommendations from your friends. You call both and set up times to meet with them, and they both seem very pleasant on the phone. When you approach the first banker, she stands, walks around from behind her desk and shakes your hand firmly. She offers you a seat and gives a great presentation on how she and her company can help grow your business for you.

You go to the second company and approach the commercial banker. He stands to greet you, but stays behind his desk, does not shake your hand, but offers you a seat. He is pleasant, gives a great presentation, and seems to have similar products and services to the other bank.

Who are you going to give your business to? Who would most people give their business to? In most cases the person who came around the desk and shook hands will get the business. The reason may be that we are going to ask ourselves a question: "Why did that one banker not shake my hand? It was a business situation, where I expected one would occur, but why didn't it? Were they uncomfortable with me for some reason? Was it the color of my skin? My age? The way I am dressed? Or, is it about them? Maybe they don't have any confidence in themselves or their products and services?"

The million-dollar question is: Do you want to do business with someone who is either uncomfortable with you, or uncomfortable with themselves? Most of us would choose not to, and we would choose another option. None of those things may be true, but once again, perception becomes our reality.

I would suggest spending some time evaluating the steps that you take each day, with each customer, and see if you can find situations where you may be leaving misperceptions. I would also work diligently to not only remove misperceptions, but also seek ways by which you can exceed your customer's expectations.

10
Life is Chaos

I AM SURE THAT MOST OF YOU KNOW BY NOW HOW CHAOTIC TODAY'S lifestyle is. It is nothing like it was 30 years ago. It requires two people to be working in most households just to be able to pay the basic bills, and sometimes even our kids are working just to help us keep up. The stress, the anxiety, and all the hassle that we deal with today are overwhelming sometimes, and it is a rare occurrence when someone shows us appreciation for that.

If you have a lifestyle like myself, or many other people, you might get up at five o'clock in the morning, get an hour workout in (if you have time), shower, get a little breakfast for yourself and get dressed. Then you get the kids up and showered, get them dressed, make them breakfast, make their school lunches, then get them off to school. You head off to work, where you sit in rush hour traffic for an hour, put in 8 hours at work and sit in rush hour traffic on the way home. You swing by the store for a few groceries, get dinner started, take one kid off to ballet, the other kid off to soccer practice, and you rush back home again to finish making dinner and get a load of laundry in the wash.

You pick up one kid at soccer practice, the other kid at ballet, get home, eat dinner, pay some bills, do some chores, watch the 10 o'clock news, see the significant other for 10 or 20 minutes, then fall asleep. You get back up the next day, and what do we do the next day? That's right . . . the same thing. That's our life! And, you know what? We all think that we're the only ones. It's like a pity party out there because we all think we are the only ones with this crazy life, and we feel sorry for ourselves. But understand, most people are living that same kind of lifestyle. Anytime you interact with an external or internal customer, please show tremendous consideration for their time, because they too have very little of it.

Acknowledging the customer quickly is the most important thing for your customer. It does not mean you have to "assist" them right away, but it is crucial to let them know that they are important, and you will be with them soon. Acknowledging customers can be verbal, or it can be non-verbal. Verbally is obviously the best answer. If you see a customer that you could acknowledge verbally, just give them good eye contact and a smile, then say; "It's good to see you today!" or "I'll be right with you!" You may use any words that verbally communicate the message; "Welcome - I see you are here."

If you're not able to verbally communicate with the customer, maybe because of the distance they are from you, then communicate using non-verbal techniques. This must include a smile, and be accompanied by either an acknowledging nod of the head, or a hand gesture (like raising an index finger) that communicates the message; "I see you, and will be with you shortly."

Have you ever been in a retail business, where you stood in the middle of the store, and watched the employees walk right past you trying not to look at you in the eyes? Did you feel like you were stealth? Remember the anxiety that you experienced, and how horrible that felt to you? Would you want to do that to anybody else? Of course not!

Acknowledging customers quickly is very important, and it should be a team effort. Even if you've got a designated person at a customer service desk in your business or environment, it is still every employee's duty to make sure each customer gets acknowledged promptly. At Disneyland, if there is a piece of paper on the ground, they do not care who picks it up, as long as somebody picks it up. Just because it is one of their duties, it does not have to only be the maintenance people who do it. Everyone in your company may have specific duties, but customer service is everyone's responsibility. It is all about creating a great experience for the customer, and that requires all employees to contribute.

When you're working with customers, there may be a circumstance when you have to excuse yourself. The customer will be accepting of this, as long as you don't do it repeatedly, and you follow four simple steps to excuse yourself properly.

1. If you know the customer's name, use it as you excuse yourself.
2. Tell the customer briefly why you need to excuse yourself.
3. Tell them about how long you're going to be.
4. Thank them upon return and use their name.

There may be many reasons you will need to remove yourself, and it may sound something like this: "Mr. Johnson, if you can excuse me, I've got to go in the backroom and locate another size for you, but I'll be back in less than a minute." And, when you return, you say, "Thank you for waiting Mr. Johnson, I found your size."

In a situation like I sampled above, you may think that being gone for a minute is not a big deal, and does not warrant excusing yourself or thanking the customer for waiting. Let's not think about what shouldn't be done; let's think about what could be done. What are we going to do that no one else is willing to do? What are we going to do to exceed each customer's expectations?

I was in Boise, Idaho performing a customer service seminar for one of my clients a few years ago. I checked into the hotel and went to the room where my seminar was going to be held. I always check to make sure that the audio system is functioning at the right level, and that the overhead projector works properly (before I began using PowerPoint). The overhead projector was not even in the room, so I went to the front desk to ask for their assistance. I told the woman at the desk that my seminar was to begin in 30 minutes, and the overhead projector was not in the room as I had requested. She never said a word. With an expressionless look, she turned, walked through a door to the backroom and disappeared. After waiting 10 minutes (and feeling my anxiety grow), a different woman came through the backroom door, smiled at me and asked if I had been helped. I told her that I was not sure if I had been helped or not, and proceeded to explain what occurred. She said she would check on the status of my overhead and then she disappeared through the same mysterious backroom door. It was 10 minutes later that the first woman reappeared and told me that they would deliver one to the room for me in the next five minutes. My seminar was to begin in 10 minutes and the room was full of people that were getting antsy.

So as you can imagine, I had a ton of anxiety, which all could have been avoided with the courtesy of communication.

It is important to understand that you can create anxiety in some customers if you don't excuse yourself and give them an approximate time frame. When you turn around and walk away from your customer without excusing yourself, you normally know where you are going and how long it will take; but they don't. Don't ever assume that the customer should know, or that we don't have the right to know. Think of the anxiety you would create for a mother that stops by for a quick transaction on their way to the daycare. She has to pick her daughter up in the next 10 minutes before her daycare closes, and then you walk away from her without excusing yourself properly and disappear in a backroom. Excusing yourself will relieve anxiety and show the customer that you have consideration for their time.

I would also suggest following these exact same steps on the telephone. If you are working with a customer, never answer a telephone until you have excused yourself properly using the same four steps. Once again, use the customer's name, tell them briefly what you need to do, and about how long you're going to be, and then thank them afterwards. As an example, you may say, "Mr. Worthley, if you will excuse me just one moment, I've got to answer this telephone call, but I'll be back with you in about 15 seconds." Answer the telephone, make it very brief, hang the telephone up, look back into the customer's eyes, and say, "Thank you Mr. Worthley for your patience, now let's continue."

Now, in your real world, does the telephone call always go that fast? Of course not! There may be a circumstance where a customer has a lot of questions, or you can see it is going to consume more of your time than anticipated. When you pick up that telephone, your goal is to probe for that customer's needs and find out immediately what they want. You may determine that you can't help that person, or that it might take a little bit longer than you have at that moment. You need to communicate immediately to the person on the telephone that you are working with another customer, but would love to call them back so you can spend more time with them. The call may sound something like this; "Mr. Johnson, I'm working with a customer at this moment, but I would love to talk to you more about your needs. Can I give you a call back in maybe 10 or 15 minutes, when I can spend more time with you?"

What message did the person on the telephone get? They heard that you are busy at that moment, but you want to spend more time with them. In short, you've just told them how valuable they are. What message did you send the person who is in front of you at that moment? You just told them that they're very important, because they're right there in front of you and they are your first priority. Whether on the telephone or in-person, both customers received a great message, which is that you have consideration for people's time.

If you do have customers who are waiting in line to be assisted, such as a teller line or grocery line, I suggest that you don't apologize to waiting customers. Instead, I suggest that you to simply thank them. Anytime you apologize to a customer; you're sending the message that you've screwed up. An apology says "We have made a mistake," and just because you're busy, you haven't done anything wrong.

Thank the customer for their wait. When a customer steps forward, look them in the eyes, smile, and say, "Thank you very much for your wait, and how may I assist you?" You may also use words that show your appreciation, such as; "I certainly appreciate your patience, now how may I assist you?" This greeting is much more positive than an apology, and shows consideration for their time.

11
Everybody Wants to Go
Where Everybody Knows Their Name

Earlier when we talked about Safeway, we talked about how critical it was to use the customer's name and how we develop an emotional bond with our customer by using their name. Remember the theme song from the television show "Cheers?" "Everybody wants to go, where everybody knows their name." Run that song through your head a few times, and you will see that it is a very true song.

Think about places that you might frequent such as restaurants, stores, or bars, where they know your name. Are you more loyal to them than to businesses that don't know you by name? I joined Gold's Gym about 10 years ago in order to get in shape. When I first walked into the gym, it was very intimidating. Most of the people I envisioned working out there were big muscle bound guys. When I walked in the door, there was a gentleman that sits behind the desk checking everyone in. When I walked in for the first time, he was greeting the members that he knew by name: "Hey Jim, Hi Bob, good to see you today Sally." All of a sudden he sees me, and he says, "Hey, you, new guy, you need a card." So, I walked over, he takes my picture, hands me a card and says, "I'm going to need to see your card everyday."

The next day, I walked in the door, he's saying hi to everybody by name again, "Hey Sam, Hi Troy, Hey Jim," and then he sees me; "Hey, I need to see your card." So, for three weeks, I was "Card Guy."

I could hear everybody else's name being used, but he kept treating me like I was an alien. Three weeks and one day later I walked in the door, and like usual, the people in front of me were greeted by name; "Hi Bob, Hey Sue, Hey Jane." Then much to my surprise, he looks up at me and says, "Hey Brad!" All of a sudden, I am one of the gang; this is my clan, these are my people, what a great place! I was no longer the alien.

Everyday as I walked in the gym door, he greeted me by name, so now other people are hearing my name as I walk in. I'm out on the gym floor working out with weights and people are walking by saying hello to me by name. What a wonderful feeling being part of a community! A couple years later, 24-hour fitness came to town and built a facility about one block away. They offered rates about half of what Gold's Gym charged in order to take their business away. Did many of the regulars leave? No, because we had our emotional attachment to Gold's Gym, where they know our name. Were we going to leave Gold's and go back to becoming "Card Guy" in another place? Not on your life!

One of my favorite restaurants is in Bellevue, Washington. It's a very small restaurant in an old part of town, and I have never seen them advertise. They have an inconspicuous street sign, and it is a small intimate setting. I only heard about it because a friend told me. It was interesting because when the friend told me about this place, they said, "You've got to go there because they have got great service." They never mentioned the food, which I found interesting.

I made reservations for 7:30 one night, and when I arrived, the owner was standing at the door, very opulently dressed and very well spoken. He asked my name, and when I told him, he responded with; "Mr. Worthley, this must be your first time here", which I responded with; "Yes, it is." He said, "Welcome, we are glad you are here." He took me and my guest to our table, offered us a seat, and came back three times during dinner. All three times when he came back to check on us, he would use my name. He would use it in conversation such as; "Mr. Worthley, are you enjoying your meal?" Or, "Mr. Worthley, do you like tonight's wine?"

I knew what he was doing, and I could see him doing it with other tables, as well. I thought that is extremely admirable that the owner would try to learn the names of his clients. I didn't realize how powerful it was until a week later when I came back in for lunch and I didn't have a reservation. I walked in the door, he looked up, and he said; "Mr. Worthley, it's good to see you back." I was blown away that he remembered me and remembered my name! I thought about how incredible it was, with all the people that he sees and meets, that he was able to remember my name. And yes, the food is fabulous as well!

There are reasons, or should I say excuses, why some people don't use the customer's names. I think one of the biggest ones I have heard over the years is; some people don't know whether to use the customer's first name or their last name. There's an unspoken rule that seems to work quite well; and that is if the customer is younger than you, you could use their first name, and if they're older than you, you use their last name out of respect. But, there may be a circumstance where you can't tell the person's age. If you cannot tell which way to go, the absolutely safest thing you can do is use the customer's last name. Whether they are 80 years old, or 8 years old, if you use their last name you're going to have a satisfied customer. Especially the 8 year old who is now extremely happy with you.

If I walked in the door, you might address me as Mr. Worthley, so that's pretty safe. But when a woman walks in the door, how do we address them if we don't know whether they are married or not? The safest way to address women is "Ms", such as; "It is good to see you Ms. Worthley." In re-lations to this issue, I get asked all the time if it is OK to use "Ma'am," and I would recommend against it as a general rule, unless you are in one of the southern states, where it is already part of the culture, and used respectfully.

Then there is the anxiety many people get when they have a customer with a difficult name to pronounce. You need to understand that everybody else is afraid of their name too and that is why these people never get to hear their names. The Smiths and the Jones of the world get to hear their name all the time. It's still pretty powerful when they hear their name being used, but the people that have the difficult names are the ones that get the most out of hearing it. Whenever you see a name that is very challenging to you, individualize and personalize that person's service by reaching out and asking them the question; "May I ask how you pronounce your name?" Or, be completely honest by saying: "That is a name I have not seen before, can you help me pronounce it?" That is something that most people aren't willing to do, and that would exceed most people's expectations.

12

Monotone is Not a
Musical Instrument

ONE OF THE WAYS THAT WE'RE JUDGED IS BY THE SINCERITY in our voice as we speak. When you're talking to a customer and you're thanking them for their business, or thanking them for coming in, make sure that you're injecting sincerity into your voice. Have you ever made a store purchase where the cashier handed you the bag and your change, then said "Thank you" in a weak monotone indifferent manner? Did you feel like they really meant it, or did they do it because it was mandated in the policy manual? You should be sincere when thanking all customers for their business, because if they stop coming in, you may not have a job.

The quality of your voice is absolutely crucial in sending the message that you truly care. You may see or talk on the phone to a hundred or more customers per day, but it may be the first time they've seen or talked to you, so don't get caught up in the sometimes lethargic behavior that results from repetition. Make sure that you're trying to inject individualized personalized service into each customer interaction by the voice that you use. Whether or not you're using the customer's name, thanking them, or asking if there is anything else you can do for them today, make sure that your voice sends the perception of sincerity.

When talking on the telephone, it is especially critical to have a friendly voice, because that is all we have to listen to. I recommend that you smile before speaking into the telephone, because we can hear the difference in your voice quality. I perform consulting and training services for people who work in call centers. In one call center, we put small mirrors up on the computer screens, so before they answered each call, we asked them to look in the mirror, smile, then answer the phone. The customers perception of the employees changed dramatically, because the smile not only made them sound friendlier, but it has been proven that smiling also releases endorphins into the brain, which make employees feel better and enjoy their work more.

If smiling and being sincere can make the customer feel better and the employees feel better, then it is a win-win. People don't care how much you know until they know how much you care. And sincerity tells them how much you truly care.

13
Can You Hear Me?

ONE OF THE MOST POWERFUL MESSAGES you can send a cus-tomer, co-worker, significant other, child, or any hu-man being, is; "I am listening." Listening has a motivating effect on people, because it leaves the perception that we care and value their opinion. It is one of the top motivators of people, even more than money or other types of financial reward.

Long ago, someone came up with a great line of ques-tioning that deals with listening, and I apologize for not knowing the source, but it goes like this:

If you want to sell your house, you talk about
your house.
If you want to sell your car, you talk about your car.
If you want to sell yourself, you talk about . . . *them.*

The reason is, that people not only love to talk about themselves (or their kids, grandkids, and pets), but they love it when someone is willing to listen. I think it is amus-ing how you can meet someone for the first time, ask them a couple questions about themselves, let them talk for 15 minutes, and when you walk away, they will tell people; "What a great guy, I really liked him!"

God gave us two ears and one mouth for a reason, because we should use them proportionately. We should listen far more than we speak, but most of us don't. This is especially true in a sales environment, where you want the customer to do most of the talking. There are a number of reasons we want the customer to be the primary speaker. One of those is that the only person that knows what they want is the customer. So the more information we can gain from them, the better we can help determine their needs. Asking superficial questions is not only useless in helping the customer, but it also sends the message that you truly don't care about the customer's needs.

There is a disease called "showing up and throwing up" that sometimes occurs in the sales world. The customer shows up and you throw up everything you know about your company and the products or services that you are selling. You not only don't get a chance to find out about the customer's needs, but you might also confuse them by overwhelming them with information. If a customer gets confused, their brain shuts down and they only have one objective - getting away from you without embarrassing themselves. A customer that is confused will not want to look dumb, so they are no longer listening to you, they are planning their escape. One of the signs of confusion can be, "Do you have a brochure that I can take with me so I can think about it?" They don't want a brochure. They want a quick escape from you.

Another reason to ask questions of the customer is a physical restriction that each human has placed upon them, and that is called the reticular activating system.

Everyone has this switch in the brain, and most of us have very little control over it because we are unaware of it. I believe that awareness creates change and being aware of this system will dramatically improve your listening and communication skills.

Do you remember sitting in a classroom in high school or college for an hour? You knew the teacher was in the room because you could see them walking around and you could also hear them talking, but you walked out of that class after an hour and had no idea what you learned? It has happened to all of us at some point and time, but most of us did not know why.

Anytime you are daydreaming or having "self-talk," which is affectionately referred to as "telling-tension," your reticular activating system will shut off like a light switch. When the switch is open, you can retain the information that you are hearing, but if it is closed, you will hear the words, but you will not retain the information. So if you are in a conversation, you need to be aware of your reticular activating system, and make sure you keep it open, otherwise you are robbing yourself of information and doing the person you are talking to a tremendous disservice by not listening to them.

It is very hard to tell if the person you are talking to has their reticular activating system open. Increase the likelihood by making sure you ask them a lot of questions in order to free up their telling-tension (by getting them to talk). Once again, this is especially true in a sales environment. The customer might have a lot of questions, and if you don't give them the opportunity to ask their questions, they will try to retain them, which is creating telling-tension (they have something to tell you, or ask you). Asking lots of questions increases the likelihood that when you are ready to speak, they will be ready to listen.

However, as you are speaking, make sure to watch the person's body language, and especially their eyes. If you are speaking and say something that confuses the person, or creates a question in their mind, they may roll their eyes upwards (they may look up in a questioning manner). When you see their eyes roll up, or turn away from you, it would be a good time to stop talking and ask the person if they have any questions. If they have a question (telling-tension), they have probably stopped listening to you, because the reticular activating system is closed, so you might as well be talking to a brick wall.

Due to the reticular activating system, and its constant

state of activity, we have three levels of listening:

LEVEL ONE LISTENING is how most people communicate because we are only retaining what we hear, or truly listening, about half the time. This happens because as someone else is talking, we are formulating a response or pondering their words. It can also occur because we are not interested in what they are saying, so we are thinking about how to get out of the conversation, or what else we should be doing (disinterest). Any self-talk will sabotage your ability to truly hear the person speaking or retain the information.

LEVEL TWO LISTENING is a deeper level of listening with very low self-talk. The reticular activating system is open and you are retaining information because you are focused on the person you are talking to and not trying to formulate a response. This is what I call "being present" in conversation, because you are sincerely listening to each word, and avoiding judgment (which creates self-talk). This is a level that takes lots of practice and is not achieved without significant thought. Very few people will ever achieve level two listening skills, because it is too hard to break our old listening habits.

LEVEL THREE LISTENING is the same as level two, but you are also listening at an intuitive level. You are hearing each word and staying present in the conversation, but you are also listening to the person's voice inflection trying to hear subtle messages. The messages might be anxiety, fear, anger, joy, passion, or many other emotions that the spoken word will not tell you about. If the person is in front of you (and not on the phone), then you would also watch their body language in order to pick up additional messages that are not in the spoken word. The highest performing sales people must communicate at level three, because that is where opportunity exists.

Being a great listener is a learned skill in most cases, and requires lots of practice, but it is well worth the effort. It separates great sales people from good sales people, great parents from good parents, great friends from good friends, great significant others from good significant others, and great leaders from good leaders.

14
Have a Good One?
Are You Kidding Me?

HAVE YOU EVER HAD A TRANSACTION WITH AN EMPLOYEE, where they took your money, gave you change, handed you your package, then said; "Have a good one!" Are you kidding me? Have a good one? What the heck does that mean, and how is that supposed to make me feel valued? And why, only one? If you really liked and appreciated me, you would have given me more than "one."

What words are we using every day that offer no added value in the customer's experience or that leave a less than desirable perception? Our goal should be to exceed the customer's expectations. So what words can we use to do that? If we want to send the customer off with a smile on their face, or with positive feelings about their experience, we should tell the customer to:

"Have a fabulous day!"
"Have a great week!"
"Enjoy the exceptional weather!"

One of my other peeves occurs after a customer thanks

an employee for helping them. At least 20% of the time, the employee will respond back with the words "No problem." That's right, the customer says "Thank you" and the employee says something like, "Oh, no problem." Do they have any idea what they have just told the customer? Maybe the customer heard, "You know what, you're not near as big a problem as I thought you were going to be!" I don't think that would exceed any customer's expectations.

I suggest you avoid the words, "No problem." Now, for those of you who are "No problemers," you know it is already a habit. You say those words automatically, and you don't even know you're saying them. It will take some time in order to remove these words from your vocabulary, but you must start today.

When someone says "Thank you" to you, what can you say to exceed their expectations? Do you think "You're welcome" would do that? "You're welcome" is a courteous response, but I don't think it would exceed anybody's expectations. Instead, I would like you to use the words, "My pleasure." Anytime a customer says "Thank you" to you, I want you to respond sincerely with "It's my pleasure." Look into their eyes and see what it does to people - it almost creates a physical transformation. People's eyes widen and they go light on their feet, because it elevates the customer's experience instantaneously.

Another consideration is when a customer says, "How

are you doing today?" Remember that this is a social pleasantry, and most customers do not actually care. If you're not feeling good, customers don't want to hear you whine. If you asked an employee that question, the last thing we want is for them to turn around and say; "Well, not bad, but I've got a rash back here on my butt the size of Texas, you ought to see this bad boy." Hey, that is way too much sharing, okay?

I had an experience at my local grocery store, one early winter Sunday morning. I stopped to buy some soft drinks for my son, and I set the six pack on the cashier's counter. She wasn't smiling and seemed rather indifferent to my existence, so I thought I would see if I could get her talking and cheer up. Boy was I sorry I did that.

I said to her, "How are you today," as a social pleasantry and an opening to get her talk. She unleashed into what had to be a two-minute tirade without taking a breath. It made me sorry I ever asked the question.

She said, "Well I wasn't bad until about six o'clock this morning, when my manager called me up and said I had to work today because Suzie wanted the day off to go skiing. So I had to get up, change all of my plans for the day in order to accommodate them. I had to hurry to make it on time and it was raining and hard to see, and I almost got hit by a truck. Then I got here to find out that I am the only cashier until noon, which infuriated me. The manager has no consideration for me and my time . . ." Two minutes later I walked out the door depressed and guilty that I bothered her.

When a customer walks in and says, "How're you doing?" Think about what you can do to put a smile on their face. What can we do or say, to make that person feel like we have exceeded their expectations, and provide them with a fun experience? I respond back with words like; "I am fabulous," or "I am lovely and thank you for asking." If something comes out of your mouth that makes the customer smile, that's a great deal!

15
Yes, We Are Judging You!

O NE OF THE TOOLS WE USE TO JUDGE EACH OTHER is our voice. When customers call your business and talk to you, your voice plays an extremely powerful role in how they judge you. Whenever we hear a flat or monotone voice on the telephone, it sends poor perceptions. For example, if I called your business, and you said in a monotone voice, "Mr. Worthley . . . we're just thrilled you called our store." Well, you might mean that, but when I hear your monotone voice, I am left with the perception that; "Mr. Worthley we can pretty much give a rip about you." Anytime customers hear a flat or monotone voice, they perceive you are either:

1. Unfriendly
2. Indifferent to helping us
3. You don't like your job

All of these or none of these may be true, but that's how flat or monotone voices are perceived. Remember, perception is the customer's reality.

Statistically, approximately 86% of how you're being judged on the telephone is your voice inflection - it is the quality of your voice. The remaining 14% of how you are judged is the actual words that you use. If I'm trying to decide if I want to drive 30 minutes down to your location to do business with you, I'm not necessarily focusing as much on your expertise (even though it is still a consideration). I'm listening to your voice to hear if you are friendly, confident, honest, compassionate, empathetic or sincere. Once again, people may not care how much you know, until they know how much you care, and that can come from your voice.

Have you ever heard your voice on a tape recorder or a camcorder before, and liked it? The first time I heard my voice, I thought "Hey, that's not me, that's Satan!" It was not good news! Changing your voice is not an easy thing to do. But, if you're going to change your voice, you've really got limited options. One of the simplest ways is to raise the volume of your voice. When you pick up a business phone, use a more powerful voice and not a soft "home" voice. When you answer with 15% or 20% more volume, it comes across as much more confident. Another option, is to change your pitch and tone. This is much more challenging and takes quite a bit more time because your voice is obviously a habit that you are comfortable with. Trying to increase your pitch and tone can sound exaggerated to you, because you are simply not used to the new you.

Even simple words can change meaning, based on how they're inflected. Let's just say I see a young lady sitting on a park bench, I walk up to her and I say, "How're you doing?" in a friendly voice. By the way I said that, with high pitch and tone in order to make it friendly, we're going to be good buddies. But, if you have ever watched the show called "Friends" and heard Joey speak to women, he would say "How you doin'," in his macho voice. Well, you know Joey probably has more on his mind than being a good buddy. Our words can take on different meanings, based on how we inflect them.

We also judge people when we are in each other's presence. We judge friends, relatives, co-workers, customers and people we don't even know. We are judging machines by nature and it isn't even a conscious effort. Our judging radar is always up and working, so it is important to know how our radar works. There are three ways that we judge each other:

1. One is what we say, which is the content of our message or the words we use.
2. The second way is how we say it. We're listening to the voice quality, for things like sincerity, humor, or compassion. So even though we're standing face to face with someone, we're still listening to the voice just as carefully as if we were on the phone with them.
3. The third way we judge people is by their appearance. In other words, we're looking at how they are dressed, at how their shoulders are rolled back with confidence or presence, or how they use

their hands to speak. We are looking at the eye contact they are providing and how high they hold their head as they speak.

All three of these things are incredibly important, and should be taken into consideration whenever we are in the presence of anyone. This is especially critical information if you are going in for a sales call, job interview, or anyplace where you need to sell yourself.

Sixty-eight percent of the people that we alienate perceive that they've been treated with indifference. That means that 68% of the people that walk away not liking us, didn't think we cared enough about them. Maybe we create some of those moments when our customers all seem to be having "bad hair days". Maybe it is us! Maybe we're having the "bad hair day" and spreading it to them. Our behavior is a direct reflection of how we want to be treated in return. Customers may be judging us by looking at our behavior, and if they perceive we are cold or indifferent, they may treat us that way in return. Put on the big smile, greet everyone warmly, maintain a friendly demeanor, and have fun at work; and you may just get it back in return. If your customers all seem in a bad mood, you better go look in the mirror, because it may be you!

What happens when the customer judges us or our business, and decides that we did not serve their needs? Ninety-seven percent of the customers unhappy with our service don't complain, they just don't return. Calculate those numbers out: If you have 3 customers who call in and complain, that means that 97 other people felt the exact same way and never told you about it, and they're not coming back. Calculate it out even further: If you have 6 customers call in to your business and complain, that means 194 other customers felt the same way, and are not returning. That's not good news.

Can any business afford to lose 100 or 200 customers per month and still stay in business – no! Never assume that just because you don't hear the yelling, that everything is okay. You will do yourself a huge favor by listening carefully to the whispers, because that is where the warning signs are.

16
Go Ahead...Make My Day!

IN THE REAL WORLD, YOU WILL PROBABLY HAVE TO DEAL with a difficult customer at some point. Most of these people are nice at heart and don't get any big kick out of giving you a "bad hair day". In most cases, if they are upset, it is because they perceive they have been "wronged" and simply want a resolution. Most are feeling like victims, and they simply want to be heard. Many times, their disposition was created before they encountered you (personal problems or prior business interaction), and you are simply in the wrong spot at the wrong time.

SCENARIO 1

Someone comes in to your business, gets in your face, and starts yelling at you. If you step over to the "dark side" with that customer and get angry back at them, you have now escalated the situation. You may now have two egos battling head to head with neither party wanting to back down. More than likely, you have probably drawn other customers and employees into observing the altercation, which makes it even harder for anyone to back down. No one wants to look wrong, or lose face in the eyes of other observers, so the chance for escalation grows dramatically.

This is a lose-lose situation that must be avoided at all costs.

SCENARIO 2

Someone comes in to your business, gets in your face, and starts yelling at you. If you can influence their life by treating them with respect and empathizing with their concerns, anger, or frustrations; who wins? Everybody wins. I truly mean everybody, because not only do you and the customer come away winners, but other customers and your co-workers see how you handled the situation and observe a happy ending. No matter how much anxiety you have over angry or difficult customers, keep your ego out of it. There is only one way to handle challenges like this; you need to treat that customer like you would want to be treated.

Please pay close attention to this sentence: "Treat a person as they are, and they will remain as they are. Treat a person as they could be, and they may become the person they should be." Basically, it says that if a customer has a bad hair day going on and you treat them like that, they're going to stay that way. Why on earth would they change? All you have done is to reinforce they have a right to act this way, because everyone around them is a jerk too. Forget how they're acting and treat them like you want them to be, because they may become the person they should be.

17

Lights – Camera – Action!

W HEN IT COMES TO EXCEEDING CUSTOMER'S EXPECTATIONS, one of the keys is the consistency with which you serve your customers. The main thing to remember is that we should treat every single person with respect, regardless of the way they are dressed, the color of their skin, whether they are tall or short, skinny or large, beautiful or ugly. Every single customer deserves 100% of your best effort, and there is no place for "time off" from outstanding customer service. If you wake up in a bad mood, don't think for a moment that you have the right to subject your customers to it. When you step into your office, store, branch, or work space, it should be "Lights – Camera – Action!" and you are on stage. Even if you are not in the best mood, your customers cannot know it. Yes, there are many days that you are going to have to "act" your way through the day, but that is what is required in order to maintain consistency.

Let's say you wait on 1,000 people a day, and you treat 999 of them really well: Is that good enough? Not if you're the one person who did not get treated well. If 99.9% is truly good enough, then that means that:

1. 2 million documents will be lost by the IRS this year.
2. 22,000 checks will be deducted from the wrong bank accounts in the next 60 minutes.
3. 1,314 calls will be misplaced by the phone company each minute.
4. 1 million credit cards are going to have the wrong cardholder info on them.
5. 12 babies will be given to the wrong parents each day.

Let's take a look at how the lack of consistency might make some customers feel alienated. For example, let's say that I stopped by my bank branch to deposit a check. I just moved to town from out of state and have been doing business with this bank for only a few months. I walk in the door and get in line behind three other customers waiting to be served. As the first customer steps forward, I hear the teller use that person's name in conversation. The second person steps forward and I hear them greeted by name, and listen to some brief social conversation between them. The person in front of me steps forward; they have a brief but friendly transaction, then as the customer walked away, the teller said; "Have a great day, Bob!" At this point, based on my observations, I am very impressed with my new bank and how friendly the people seem to be. Now I step forward, hand the teller my check and they don't use my name.

The teller may be thinking that they used three out of

four customer's names, which is great. In baseball terms, they would be hitting 750, which is incredible and should be rewarded, but not in the world of customer service. Guess how that teller made me feel by not using my name? I'm now wondering, "What's wrong with me? Why did you choose to use everyone else's name but mine?" The consistency with which you do things is crucial; otherwise, you may end up alienating some customers.

When it comes to consistency, you should also pay attention to gender. If a man and a woman are walking toward you in a business environment, whose hand are you going to shake first? It's not really important whose hand you shake first, as long as you offer it to both. Personally, it is whoever gets in my space first; whoever got closest to me. I would offer them the handshake first, but I would always offer it to the other person as well and never try to outguess who is the power in the couple (in a personal or professional setting).

If you are working with a couple, make sure to keep your eye contact between the two balanced and consistent. In reality, it may not take very long to figure out who is the dominant one between the couple, by their body language. When you ask a question of the couple, such as, "How may I help you folks?" Sometimes you can see somebody's head directing traffic for you, trying to show you where the power in the relationship is. Don't fall into the trap of abandoning that person who is directing you. People that are inadvertently helping you out by showing you where the power is, are not asking to be abandoned. It takes a tremendous amount of discipline to keep your eyes on them. No matter where the power is coming from, keep your eyes going back and forth and keep it balanced. If you don't know this already, at least 65% of the family purchasing decisions are made by women.

18

Small Changes - Big Improvements

PRESENTLY, YOU MAY BE VERY SUCCESSFUL in your job and with your customer service skills. But like standing in a telephone booth with only 49 cents - look how much more successful you could be with that one extra penny. It's not the big things that are needed in order to create big change. The key is to commit to some change. Otherwise, you will always be limited to the results you have today.

Begin doing three things tomorrow that you did not do today. I'm not talking about big monumental things; I'm talking about little things that make big differences. I'm talking about using the words, "My pleasure" when someone thanks you. Maybe you will commit to being more consistent about some of the things you do. Maybe you will begin using the customer's name in conversation in order to help create a more emotional attachment with them. Choose three things that you know you can successfully accomplish and reward yourself for a job well done. Once those three things have become part of your routine and ingrained into your culture, choose three more things.

19
Other Great "Wow" Stories

THE DISNEY DIFFERENCE: One of my loyal newsletter readers, Amy Pierce, offered a story about her trip to Disneyland, and I want to share the short version with you: Her family had finished a day at Disneyland and was waiting for a shuttle at the Disney Hotel to take them back to the airport to head home. Her 3 year old daughter was very tired and in serious need of a nap. A Disney character, which was blowing up balloon characters, made her a balloon dog which thrilled her and kept her entertained.

As they walked out of the hotel lobby to wait for their shuttle, a gust of wind blew the 3 year olds balloon out of her hand and across the loading area. She screamed "My dog, my dog!" The bellmen all dropped their luggage and ran to catch the balloon for the little girl. It got stuck under a van and popped from the heat of the vehicle, which put the poor little girl into hysterics.

The bellman apologized profusely and said he would try to find another one, but Amy told him it was no big deal and that her daughter was simply tired. Five minutes later, the bellman approaches them and hands the 3 years old a

12" Minnie Mouse doll from the gift shop. He said, "I just could not let your experience end this way." They have been back three times because one employee created a lifetime customer.

THE TOP FOODS EXPERIENCE: A client of mine told me about their trip to the grocery store recently, which began as a disaster, and turned into a great customer service experience. He had pulled into the parking lot of a Top Foods Grocery Store, and as he got out, he noticed gas spewing from underneath the car (an apparent leak near the fuel pump). A large puddle was quickly forming under the car, and all it would have taken was a lit cigarette tossed his direction to create a horrific scene.

In a panic, he ran into the store, found a clerk and hurriedly asked him for kitty litter to help soak up his gas, and to have them please call a tow truck quickly. The clerk ran and grabbed a couple bags of kitty litter, and then dashed to my friend's car where he spread the litter over the gas puddle.

While they were waiting for the tow truck to arrive, and his wife to come pick him up, the store employee even offered to buy him a cup of coffee to help calm him down (which he graciously accepted). My friend went to pay the clerk for the two bags of litter and they would not take his money. They treated him like a "guest" and left him with an incredible memory of his Top Foods trip, and a great story of uncommon courtesy.

THE ST. REGIS EXPERIENCE: A friend and her family stayed at the St. Regis Monarch Beach Resort & Spa during a short three day stay in Southern California. My friend was walking through the halls of the gorgeous hotel looking for an ATM machine. She passed by a hotel employee, going the opposite direction, who asked if she could help her with anything. My friend mentioned that she was looking for an ATM. The worker spun around quickly and said she would take her to it. When my friend said that she could just point it out and she could find it, the employee said; "It would be my pleasure to take you there."

Later that day by the swimming pool my friend saw a hotel employee walking towards her who she assumed was a waiter from the bar, so she flagged him down and ordered a drink. The employee said, "It would be my pleasure" and left to get the drink. She found out later he did not work in the bar, but all employees are told to do whatever it takes to serve the customer regardless of your title or duty.

When the family got home from their trip, they realized that one of them had forgotten a sweater in the room when they checked out. They called the hotel, located the sweater, and asked for it to be shipped back to Seattle. My friend offered their federal express number or a credit card number to pay for the shipping, but the hotel said it would be their pleasure to return it. It arrived via UPS in a couple days and the hotel paid for the shipping. This is a hotel that understands how to serve and make you feel valued.

THE LEXUS EXPERIENCE: A friend of mine drives a Lexus, and when she goes in to get her car serviced, she says the experience makes her feel like a princess each time. When she arrives at the service center, they immediately open her car door for her, and she is greeted by name.

When she gets to the service counter, they also greet her by name and welcome her back in. She is offered coffee, a place to sit in the waiting area, and something to read to help pass the time. She says it seems like everyone knows her name, and they use it during her entire visit to personalize the experience.

This particular Lexus dealership has put excellent systems in place to create a great experience. They enter her license plate into their computer as soon as she drives up to access her name and needs. They educate everyone to her arrival and the service "experience" begins. What systems do you have in place to create a great "experience"?

NORDSTROM: I friend of mine had received a lot of clothes for their birthday, and needed to return some of the merchandise in order to exchange some sizes. They went to the Nordstrom store, where most of the merchandise was purchased. They found a salesperson who volunteered to help them get the proper sizes.

In the process of going through the bag full of clothes, the salesperson found a pair of pants that were purchased at another store just a couple doors down from Nordstrom. My friend was in the dressing room trying different sizes on, so the salesperson said he would be back in 5 minutes. When he came back he handed my friend the pair of pants from another store and they were now the right size. He had walked down to the store while my friend was busy, and exchanged the size for him for his convenience. My friend rarely shops anywhere else but Nordstrom and normally calls ahead to make sure "his salesperson" is there to assist him. That is a win-win!

BENIHANA: Going to the Benihana restaurant in downtown Seattle is always a treat, because they put on quite a show in the process of feeding you. They provide great food and spend extra energy winning the parent's hearts, by winning over the kids. It is one of the few places I have seen where young kids are not bored and wanting to go home NOW!

I friend of mine had dinner with their family, and had some extra food left over, so they had the food put into a bag to take home. In all of the chaos of getting everyone rounded up and out of the restaurant, they had forgotten their take-home bag, but had not noticed it. The parking garage is quite a ways from the restaurant, through a maze of hallways and stairs. They got to their car, and were just starting to pull away, when they heard someone yelling. Chasing after them was a waiter waving their bag and trying to get them to stop. It would have been very easy to let them drive away and throw the bag away, but

ARE YOU WILLING TO DO THE UNORDINARY TO ACHIEVE THE EXTRAORDINARY?

that one act, has created a life-long customer, and separates them from other restaurants.

THE BROWN BAG CAFÉ: The Brown Bag Café is in Kirkland Washington, not far from my house. I had never been there before until I had a couple people mention how great it was, so I decided to go there for breakfast a few weeks ago. I walked in the door and all three people at the reception area greeted me warmly (not just the hostess, but all of them). As I was being seated, I noticed a young man cleaning a child's high chair, and he just didn't brush the crumbs off, he thoroughly wiped it all down (parents can appreciate this).

The same gentleman was my waiter and he came to my table with a huge smile and warm greeting. I noticed that all of the wait staff were smiling, happy, and seemed to enjoy their job. I asked for a couple of his favorite choices on the menu because the selection was so great, and I ordered Corn

Beef Hash which he said is the best anywhere.

He was right, the meal looked all hand cut, and the plate was heaped from rim to rim. The portions were huge, and the food was far and above the best breakfast I had had in a long time. Even the sourdough toast was twice as thick as in any other restaurant and incredibly fresh. This was better than homemade.

In every aspect of my visit, they exceeded my expectations: The greeting, service, selection, portions and quality. This is a great example of a business that got it all right, and did not try to rely simply on one or two "Wows" to separate them from the competition – they put it all out there. Their reward is that they are packed most meal times.

MY SQUIRE SHOP DAYS: About 25 years ago when I was manager of a retail clothing store named Squire Shop, I made a customer service decision that taught me a huge lesson. My store was in a mall and the store right next to us, was Sears. A gentleman around 60 years old came in and wanted to return a pair of jeans that he said his wife bought at our store. I informed him that our store had never carried that brand, and that Sears is the only store that does carry them. The man's voice got louder and his demands became greater as he continued to defend his position.

Instead of continuing to argue, I asked him if he wanted cash back or an exchange, and he said he needed about

5 pair of jeans and just wanted to exchange them. I then agreed to take them back and credit him for the $19.95 he paid (at Sears). He bought 5 pair of jeans, 3 shirts and a belt which totaled almost $200, walked away happy and continued to be a customer for years. Are you willing to do the unordinary to achieve the extraordinary?

20
Summary

A S YOU HAVE BEEN READING THIS BOOK, your reticular activating system has been going on and off as you discuss the contents of the book with yourself, or get distracted by your surroundings and you lose your attention span. This does not make you a bad reader or disinterested, it makes you human. I would highly recommend reading the book again and using a colored highlight pen to mark the issues that you find important to you. Highlighting will allow you to review the book again in the future and not have to read each word. You can focus your reading and keep your reticular activating system open so that you can retain more of what you read. I have taken one major point from each chapter of the book and written them in below for your convenience. These, however, are issues that I believe are important, but your issues may be different, so that is why I would encourage you to highlight your own as well. The following is a summary of the key points to the book:

1. Everything is a choice, and with choice comes either rewards or consequences.
2. The words you choose to use will empower or disable you, so choose them wisely.

3. Your old habits will keep you small – Break them and create positive new habits.

4. Be authentic with yourself and choose jobs that best suit your talents and passions.

5. The better you treat the customer, the better they will treat you in return.

6. Avoid the "Dark Side." No one can give you anxiety; you give it to yourself.

7. Don't talk about how good you are; show them!

8. You can no longer just meet the customer's expectations, you must exceed them.

9. Think like a customer (TLC) - Do not leave any misperceptions.

10. Show consideration and reduce anxiety in customers with prompt acknowledgments.

11. Use the customer's name in conversation to help create an emotional attachment.

12. Make sure each word which is spoken is done with sincerity.

13. Listening has a motivating effect on people. It says "We value your opinion."

14. Avoid slang and use words that exceed customer expectations.

15. The customer is judging you primarily by what they see and what they hear.

16. Treat a person as they are, and they will remain as they are. Treat a person as they could be, and they may become the person they should be.

17. Be consistent about the service you offer and

treat each person with respect.

18. Change is about small steps which lead to big improvements.

19. Always look for ways to raise the service bar – Never accept the status quo.

20. Being the best at customer service is not a destination, it is a journey – Enjoy the journey!

PERSONAL ACTION PLAN

A S WE DISCUSSED EARLIER IN THE BOOK, breaking old habits and creating positive new ones is very challenging. Once most people finish a book, it goes on the shelf with all the other great books, and most of what you learned is relegated to old memories. If you continue to do the things you are doing today, you will be limited to the results you have today. So if you plan on making noticeable changes, and using this book to catapult yourself beyond your competition, you need to commit in writing to change. Based on what you learned from reading this book, I would like you to commit to change by answering the following questions:

PERSONAL ACTION PLAN
List 3 things you can begin doing immediately.
I will START doing:

1.

2.

3.

List 1 to 3 things you should stop doing to create a better customer experience.
I will STOP doing:

1.

2.

3.

List 1 to 3 things you can continue doing that exceed customer expectations.
I will KEEP doing:

1.

2.

3.

Please look at these commitments each and every work day for the next month so that you stay focused on your goals.

Change requires focus and repetition, so use this personal action plan to forward your actions. You can create a new action plan each month if you choose, and this will help drive positive long lasting change.

About the Author

Brad Worthley is the founder and CEO of Brad Worthley International, Inc., a Bellevue, Washington based consulting, coaching and training firm. An accomplished consultant with over 31 years of business management experience, he is also an internationally acclaimed leadership and customer service expert. He has trained hundreds of thousands of people throughout a wide range of industries. A true professional, Brad equips companies with dynamic customer service and leadership essentials. He teaches leading corporations how to consistently build and retain customer loyalty using his proven methods.

Brad is also the creator of a revolutionary new concept in modifying behavior called "Perception Awareness Training." This method keeps seminar participants entertained while helping them retain the information they learn. He is a master storyteller and delivers his powerful message from the customer's perspective with sincerity and humor. Many have referred to his lively presentations as "shows." Brad is always one of the highest rated speakers at any event he speaks at, and the common response from attendees is; "I know what to do with the information Brad taught me, and I can begin using it immediately."

After college and an Associate of Science degree, Brad started his business career at the age of 20 by opening a sporting goods store. Since then, he has created and sold six other very successful businesses in the fields of retail, wholesale, marketing, distribution and consulting. He has experienced every aspect of the business world, and not only talks the talk, but walks the walk.

Brad Worthley International produces training videos and DVD's on customer service and leadership which are being used by companies of all sizes throughout the world, as well as multiple CDs and books. Brad writes articles for many business publications throughout the U.S. on customer service and leadership. In addition, he writes two monthly electronic newsletters called "Insights and Strategies" which have thousands of loyal subscribers in over 40 countries (you can subscribe at www.BradWorthley.com)

Brad is a past President (2002/2003) of the Mystery Shopping Providers Association, whose goal is dedicated to improving customer service. He received the "Volunteer of the Year Award" for 2001, and in 2002 was honored with the "Hall of Fame Award," the highest honor in the industry.

In his spare time, Brad has been a volunteer coach of youth sports for over 10 years (soccer, baseball and basketball). He donates his time speaking to high school kids as part of a program called "Washington Business Week," which helps educate students to the business world. Brad also volunteers at a domestic violence shelter for women and children one day a week.

For more information, articles and resources, visit
Brad Worthley on-line at www.BradWorthley.com

Seminars & Keynotes

☐ **Exceeding Customer Expectations** *(Internal & External)*
1 to 3 Hours: Businesses can no longer have the goal of meeting the customer's expectations; the goal today must be to exceed them. What does that look like from the customer's perspective? Brad will entertain you with great stories and hilarious examples of businesses that step out of the box and find ways to wow the customer. You will walk away with actionable information with which to make changes yourself. Targeted to anyone, from any industry, at any level. Benefits from this seminar will include:

> Increased employee performance
> Increased employee retention
> Increased customer retention
> Increased sales
> Increased profits

Key Presentation Points: Creating an emotional attachment, Perception is the customer's reality, Opening the customer's mind, Pedestal words, How people judge us, Consistency, Gender.

☐ **Outstanding Leadership in a Service Culture**
1 to 3 Hours: Are you the kind of leader that asks: "Did my employees do what they were supposed to do today?" or are you the kind of leader that asks: "Did I do what I was supposed to do today, so that my employees could do what they were supposed to do?" Brad offers thoughts on how we can change our behavior just slightly, in order to greatly impact the people we lead. This session is a must for a strong company culture. Targeted to anyone, from any industry, who supervises people. Benefits from this seminar will include:

> Eliminate office politics
> Increased employee performance
> Increased employee retention

Increased sales

Increased profits

Key Presentation Points: Walk the walk, Coach instead of teach, Synergy, Credible leadership, Giving constructive feedback, Manager styles, Learning styles, Body language, Boundaries, Motivators, De-motivators.

☐ **Changing Cultures and Not Just People**

1 Hour: Companies spend a lot of time trying to change employees, but maybe it's not them who need to change? Changing people is frustrating and an endless futile process until the culture of the entire organization has changed. Brad will offer ideas on how to make them become reality. Targeted to upper level management (decision makers). Benefits from this seminar will include:

Attitude vs. aptitude

The experience

Open dialogue

The customer's perspective

Changing your vocabulary

Employees active in the process

Accountability

Inspect what you expect

Personal action plans.

Key Presentation Points:

People don't fail, systems do - Accountability - Inspect what you expect - Re-think your role as a manager - Proactive leadership - Non-negotiable standards - Personal action plans.

☐ **Reduce Stress: Bring Balance To Your Life**

1 Hour: Improving work performance and employee morale comes with finding balance in your personal and professional life. You cannot help others if you are not able to take care of yourself, so learn how to take better care of your emotional, physical, spiritual and intellectual needs. Targeted to anyone, from any industry, who supervises people. Benefits from this seminar will include:

Reduce chaos in your life

Reduce stress

Increased employee performance

Increased employee retention

Key Presentation Points: Reduce Chaos, Motivation to Change, Prioritize Yourself, 12 Categories to Balance, Why we get out of Balance, Seeing the Big Picture, Celebrate the Small Victories.

☐ **Exceeding Customer Expectations in a Call Center World**
1 to 3 Hours: Call Centers can longer allow mediocrity in their workplace. The goal of each employee should be to "exceed" each customer's expectations and create a great experience for them. What does that call sound like from the customer's perspective? Brad will entertain you with great stories and hilarious examples of businesses that found ways to wow the customer. You will walk away with actionable information with which to make immediate changes. Targeted to anyone, at any level, in call centers. Benefits from this seminar will include:

Increased employee performance

Increased employee retention

Increased customer retention

Increased sales

Increased profits

Key Presentation Points: Creating an emotional attachment, Perception is the customer's reality, How do people judge us, Becoming an advocate, Teamwork, Attitude/aptitude, Obstacles to listening, Listening statements, Customer behaviors, Difficult customers, Sincerity, Customer Peeves, Stress.

☐ **Exceeding Customer Expectations:**
Bringing Sales and Service Together
1 to 3 Hours: Many people believe that sales and service are two separate functions, and treat them that way. This session will change the way you think, and make them a single process. You will learn how to exceed the customer's expectations, build an emotional attachment with them, and also learn how to close the sale with very little extra effort. Targeted to internal or external sales cultures, from any industry, at any level. Benefits from this seminar will include:

Increased employee performance
Increased employee retention
Increased customer retention
Increased sales
Increased profits

Key Presentation Points: Create more sales time, How to Wow them, Perception is the customer's reality, Opening the customer's mind, Pedestal words, How people judge us, Becoming a consultant, Explore their mind, Defining Value, The word No, Body language, Empowerment with options.

Call 425-957-9696 for more information on live seminars

Products Available to Help
Create and Sustain a Service Culture

Videos and DVDs

Once live training seminars have been completed, you will want new employees to step into the culture and be up to speed on the first day. That's why we offer a variety of training videos and DVDs. Video training offers a value and is critical in improving employee behavior. *The following titles are available in Video or DVD format.*

☐ **Tellers & Outstanding Customer Service**
Bank Training
In an actual bank setting, we use actors to demonstrate some of the less than desirable Teller behaviors that are commonly seen in banks or check cashing/payday loan outlets, then show how they should be done in order to exceed customers' expectations with outstanding customer service.
26 minutes long. Price $195 each

☐ **The Platform & Outstanding Customer Service**
Bank Training
In an actual bank setting, we use actors to demonstrate some of the less than desirable Platform (sales and customer service) behaviors that are commonly seen in banks, then show how they should be done in order to exceed customers' expectations and close the sale.
40 minutes long. Price $295 each

☐ **Outstanding Customer Service - Hospitality Training**
In live seminar format, Brad answers all the questions as to "Why should I change my behavior?" This video is a must for ALL industries and businesses that want to motivate employees to perform at a higher level. This motivational video will inspire everyone.
50 minutes long. Price $295 each

☐ **Outstanding Customer Service - Quick Service Restaurants**
In live seminar format, Brad answers all the questions for this industry as to "Why should I change my behavior?" It covers how to exceed customer's expectations and looks in-depth at how your employees are being perceived by the customer.
52 minutes long. Price $295 each

☐ **Outstanding Customer Service - Quick Service Restaurants**
(In English and Spanish)
In live seminar format, Brad answers all the questions for this industry as to "Why should I change my behavior?" It covers how to exceed customer's expectations and looks in-depth at how your employees are being perceived by the customer.
The video features Victor Villarreal translating to Spanish.
81 minutes long. Price $395 each

☐ **Outstanding Leadership - Step Outside The Box**
In live seminar format, Brad provides anyone in a leadership role, the tools with which to alter their behavior slightly in order to greatly impact the people they lead. This is a must for making long-term commitments to a culture change. This video is the foundation for a solid customer service strategy.
76 minutes long. Price $395 each

Audio CDs

CDs offer the same powerful seminar content and message as in live performances and in videos, but at a fraction of the cost. They can also be listened to in the car or on portable stereos, so they may provide more convenient learning for some people.

☐ **Exceeding Customer Expectations**
Businesses can longer have the goal of meeting the customer's expectations; the goal today must be to exceed them. What does that

look like from the customer's perspective? Brad will entertain you with great stories and hilarious examples of businesses that step out of the box and find ways to wow the customer. You will walk away with actionable information with which to make changes yourself. Targeted to anyone, from any industry, at any level.
65 minutes long. Only $29.95

☐ **Outstanding Leadership in a Service Culture**
Are you the kind of leader that asks: "Did my employees do what they were supposed to do today?" or are you the kind of leader that asks: "Did I do what I was supposed to do today, so that my employees could do what they were supposed to do?" Brad offers thoughts on how we can change our behavior just slightly, in order to greatly impact the people we lead. This session is a must for a strong company culture. Targeted to anyone, from any industry, who supervises people.
57 minutes long. Only $29.95

☐ **Reduce Stress: Bring Balance to Your Life**
Improving work performance and employee morale comes with finding balance in your personal and professional life. You cannot help others if you are not able to take care of yourself, so learn how to take better care of your emotional, physical, spiritual and intellectual needs.
41 minutes long. Only $29.95

☐ **Conversational Charisma – Get What You Want in Life**
Being a great communicator and getting people to develop an emotional attachment to you, is more about "attitude" than "aptitude". This CD will help you develop the skills to be a great communicator, whether it is for sales, service, leadership, relationships, or politics. You can immediately change people's perception of you with just a little fine tuning and this CD will provide you with the tools to make those changes.
50 minutes long. Only $29.95

☐ **Bringing Sales & Service Together**
Many people believe that sales and service are two separate functions, and treat them that way. This session will change the way you think, and make them a single process. You will learn how to exceed the customer's expectations, build an emotional attachment with them, and also learn how to close the sale with very little extra effort. Targeted to internal or external sales cultures, from any industry, at any level.
Two CD set – 107 minute run time. Only $49.95

☐ **14 CD & 1 DVD Leadership Series:** Motivation & inspiration from today's top success coaches such as Zig Ziglar, Brian Tracy, Jim Rohn, Chris Widener and Brad Worthley . It's a multi-session leadership retreat in a box. The leadership audio suite offers you hours of inspirational and practical steps to power-up your influence in all areas of the workplace and beyond. This 13 CD set comes with a bonus DVD from the master himself, Zig Ziglar. It comes with a compact and convenient carry case for easy travel.
Over $350 worth of CDs and a DVD for only $49.95

Visit our web-site to purchase any of of our Videos, CDs or DVDs

www.BradWorthley.com

www.BradWorthley.com